D1577699

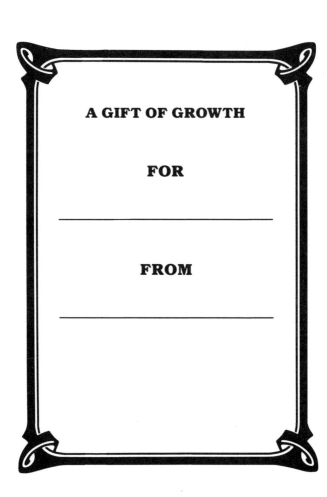

A GIFT OF GROWTH

FOR

_____

FROM

_____

A GIFT OF GROWTH

"GIFTS OF GROWTH"

Books Available

DETACHMENT
Seven Simple Steps

●

ENABLING

●

MY FIRST NINETY DAYS

Distributed by
PERRIN & TREGGETT
P.O. Box 190
Rutherford, NJ 07070
1-800-321-7912

DETACHMENT
Seven Simple Steps

1
GO FIND THE EXPERTS

2
TAKE AN INVENTORY

3
REPORT YOUR DIAGNOSIS

4
FOCUS ON YOURSELF

5
DISCOVER YOUR BOTTOM LINE

6
MAKE A DECISION

7
TAKE CHARGE OF YOUR LIFE

DETACHMENT
Seven Simple Steps

by

JUDITH M. KNOWLTON
and
REBECCA D. CHAITIN

QUOTIDIAN
Delaware Water Gap
Pennsylvania, 18327

ISBN 0-934391-00-9
FIRST EDITION
Third Printing—1987

QUOTIDIAN
1987

CONTENTS

INTRODUCTION
It's Going To Take Time!

Detachment isn't something you can learn instantaneously and permanently. Like sobriety, it will come gradually, often painfully, and not always smoothly. But it is not a mystery. It is a manageable, orderly process.

Like many of us, you probably walked into your first Al-Anon meeting exploding with frustration, anger and pain. And when you tried to unload some of it, chances are one of the old-timers told you, "But you've got to detach . . .!" So you backed off, confused and hurt, perhaps believing you had been advised to *ignore* the alcoholic in your life and stifle your own misery.

THAT'S NOT DETACHMENT! Squashing yourself and your feelings is a form of denial, and the pressure of your unresolved anger and pain can only hurt you and everyone around you.

If you're new and overwhelmed and someone tells you abruptly to detach, you might respond with, "You're right, I need to do that, but it'll take time -- and I don't want to stuff my feelings." That should be a good reminder for you and still keep the lines of communication open.

Detachment is many different things, as you will learn in this book. It is a gradual discovery of the truth about the family disease of alcoholism. It is the process of learning to see things objectively. It is learning to "unhook" yourself emotionally from the alcoholic system. And it is learning at last to act in your own best interest -- what's good for YOU -- instead of constantly reacting to whatever the alcoholic does.

The result is a new, life-giving attitude. Without it you will stay mired in the destructiveness of the alcoholic system, unable to breathe or take effective action. With it you are on the road to recovery, to emotional health, and the alcoholic's own chances to recover will improve enormously.

NOTES

STEP ONE
Go Find the Experts

You can begin the process of detachment by making a commitment to attend Al-Anon meetings regularly. There you will find love and support and the experts to help you manage your own life. Remember, they've been there!

Get an Al-Anon sponsor. Look for someone with experience and a positive, no-nonsense attitude, who sees the Twelve Suggested Steps as an ACTIVE program of recovery. Find a person you can talk to on a regular basis, preferably every single day at first.

Plan to attend an open A.A. meeting at least once a month. There you will learn how the alcoholic thinks and what motivates him.* A.A. members are the experts on how alcoholism feels FROM THE INSIDE. You'll discover much about the alcoholic in your life by listening to others tell their stories. Even your anger and resentment may dissipate as you gain compassion and objectivity. And in A.A. you'll learn about the joys of recovery and sobriety.

At these meetings, pick up pamphlets and books. Call local and regional

---

*Don't take "him" too literally. It can just as easily be "her."

alcoholism information numbers -- especially the National Council on Alcoholism in your area -- and ask to be put on mailing lists. Look under "Alcoholism" in the yellow pages of your phone book for other agencies. Collect magazine articles, go to seminars, check the library. Begin by looking for the titles listed in the back of this book. In short, GET INFORMED! If this were any other chronic, progressive, potentially fatal disease, you would need no urging!

Once you start educating yourself, you will begin to see that you are dealing not with a moral problem, but with a disease that has predictable symptoms. And that's a giant first step toward detachment!

You may want to make an appointment to talk with a professional about the disease. If you do, be certain that the person has been adequately trained in the treatment of alcoholism. Your Al-

Anon and A.A. friends will have good recommendations about local experts, and also whom to avoid. Trust their judgment.

At A.A. and Al-Anon meetings, talk to experienced members (you'll soon learn to spot them) rather than staying with other newcomers who are probably just as confused and uncertain as you. This is called "sticking with the winners", and it's *not* snobbery. It's a vital part of your learning process.

When you meet these people, share experiences, ask questions and GET THEIR PHONE NUMBERS. You are building a support network that will serve you well, and you're *coming out of the isolation that has kept you sick!*

Since alcoholism *is* a treatable disease and not a moral weakness, there are people around you who have a legitimate need to know what you've learned. There will come a time for you to share your discoveries with your children and other close relatives and friends.

NOTES

STEP TWO

Take an Inventory

This is a twist on Al-Anon's well-known admonition to "*stop* taking his inventory", by which they mean, quite rightly, to stop condemning the alcoholic's behavior while refusing to examine your own.

When we suggest that you *start* taking his inventory, we mean something very different. Start looking at his drinking *objectively*, and pay attention to recurring patterns. No judgments. No blame. Your ultimate aim is a clear-eyed look at the disease process.

For this you'll need a notebook. It will help you to maintain your objectivity and to spot the patterns. Pay particular attention to the things that seem to trigger drinking episodes. Describe the changes you see in behavior and attitudes. For example, does he pick fights as an excuse to slam out of the house to drink? Does he seesaw between remorse and resentment, or between grandiose expansiveness and utter gloom?

Learn to recognize memory lapses. This alcoholic amnesia may last for moments or even hours or days. The alcoholic appears to behave "normally", but doesn't recall what happened. We call these lapses "blackouts". Does he fish around for clues about what happened the night before, or try to pretend he remembers all about it when he obviously doesn't? Or does he greet the dawn cheerfully after last night's debacle, genuinely puzzled to find you in turmoil?

When you start observing these patterns and writing down the incidents, include the time of day, date and place. Remember that your goal is to keep a clear and accurate record -- what you SEE, not what you INTERPRET! You are learning to move away from making judgments and toward making a diagnosis. The list of twelve questions in the back of the book will help you to recognize alcoholic behavior patterns, and at some point you will accept them as recurring symptoms of a chronic and progressive disease.

NOTES

STEP THREE

Report Your Diagnosis

Your next step is to find a receptive, knowledgeable listener -- a trusted friend in A.A. or Al-Anon, your sponsor or a counselor with alcoholism training -- and describe what you have seen. (This should be done in private. You will need to ventilate some feelings, and an Al-Anon meeting is NOT the place for it!)

Choose your listener with care. When you report your observations for the first time, some of those rotten feelings are bound to pour out of you. Your listener must be able to function as a calm, non-judgmental sounding board; anyone who sees alcoholism as a moral issue obviously won't do. Once you've started "dumping the garbage", you will begin to gain objectivity about your situation, and talking about it rationally will become a lot easier.

As your objectivity -- and emotional detachment, which may be the same thing -- increases, you'll find your own residual denial beginning to crumble. But this happens slowly. You may catch yourself thinking, "Maybe it really *is* my fault, like he's always saying; maybe if I were different, he wouldn't have to drink . . ." Baloney! Once you start observing an alcoholic with a clear eye, you'll see that he really *does* have a disease -- an inexorable and progressive disease that follows certain patterns *no matter what you do!*

YOU ARE NOT THE CAUSE, and you no longer have to bear the burden of tying yourself (and everyone around you) in knots in order to "make" him stop drinking.

NOTES

STEP FOUR
Focus on Yourself

You probably realize by now that the alcoholic's illness is not your fault, but you may not be fully aware of the damage done to you. Indeed, as you will hear at meetings, *you are sick too.* And who wouldn't be? It is normal to behave abnormally in an abnormal situation! Look at it another way: you've spent all that emotional energy trying to make things right, and *it has not worked!* Your life has been so focused on him and his disease, you probably don't even know what your own needs are, much less what you *want* for yourself.

You *must* focus on yourself to survive. Begin by getting into the Al-Anon program in depth. And don't hide your involvement in Al-Anon by attending meetings only when the alcoholic is out of the house! No speeches, but he needs to know that you are working on *your* recovery. Keep in touch with your sponsor, which means calling early and often, preferably *before* a crisis. Don't wait until after disaster strikes.

It is time to work Al-Anon's Twelve Steps in earnest, with emphasis on Steps Four and Five.* Both steps will chip away at your denial and allow you

---

*The Twelve Steps are in the back of this book.

to focus on yourself. Remember to take the old-timers' suggestion to heart: don't acknowledge a defect in yourself until you can balance it with an asset. Putting yourself down isn't honest or true. Labeling yourself as worthless is a way of staying irresponsible!

As you work the Steps and start "unhooking" from the alcoholism, keep asking yourself, "What do *I* want?" For example, you might practice statements like: "I want to live in a sober environment"; "I want to stop accepting unacceptable behavior"; "I want to feel good about myself." (If your statement begins with, "I want HIM to . . .", stop right there. You're on the wrong track!)

By focusing on *your* wants and needs, and what you can *do* for yourself, you avoid a lot of pitfalls, such as trying to follow the dictates of a society that doesn't understand alcoholism, giving in to martyrdom (a real temptation, because you'll be praised for it by those who don't know better!), or trying to force the alcoholic to straighten out. All of these are surely exercises in futility.

When you focus on yourself in a positive, growth-oriented way, you get back all the emotional energy you've been investing so uselessly in the alcoholic. And heaven knows, you need it!

STEP FIVE

Discover Your Bottom Line

This is a tough step, and it may take you several months. Don't rush it. Discovering your bottom line means making an honest, realistic determination of *what you will no longer put up with and what you will do about it.* You'll need to examine alternatives very carefully, and go over them at length with an experienced counselor or Al-Anon member. For anyone who has spent years reacting to the over-whelming destructiveness of alcohol-ism -- dreading the worst, shouldering the blame, swallowing the pain, being battered or verbally abused -- this is both difficult and crucial.

Think out possible bottom lines care-fully, and *don't use them to manipu-late the alcoholic!* They have to be designed for *you,* in your own best interest. Above all, *don't threaten any-thing you're not prepared to carry through!*

Bottom lines, incidentally, are not just the big moves for dealing with the alco-holism "once and for all". They come in all sorts of everyday sizes too. You can make some positive, goal-setting bottom lines for yourself, such as: I will attend *no fewer* than three Al-Anon meetings each week; I will talk to someone in the program *daily;* I will remember to do something good for myself *every day.*

When you examine bottom lines in relation to the alcoholic, start by considering a small one you know you can stick to rather than one you might have to back away from later. Suppose, for example, that you've been filling your head with panic and projections about what he's up to, or what will become of him, or what will become of *you,* or what will the neighbors think! *This is useless, gut-churning, obsessive thinking,* and it leaves you drained and helpless. So, next time you catch yourself wallowing in the woe, you might declare a bottom line that says, "I will NOT indulge myself in this, I will call my sponsor right now" (or make plans with a friend, or simply leave the house). As you will discover, once you refocus your attention on your own needs and wants, the obsessive thinking begins to fade away.

At some point down the line, you may well conclude that you can no longer accept the drinking at all. The more detached you have become, the more clearly you will see what your options are.

STEP SIX
Make a Decision

This step is a natural outgrowth of the previous one. It's almost impossible to separate them, because by now you have begun to *act for yourself*. You are gradually detaching from the alcoholic system and its twisted, blame-oriented thinking, and you have examined many bottom lines. You are already making small, satisfying decisions. You may have found your confidence increasing as you put your bottom lines into practice. It has become much easier to deliberate, to decide, to do! You are at last ready to declare: BEYOND THIS I WILL NOT GO, PERIOD!

Again, make your choices carefully. No one else, no matter how experienced or empathetic, can choose your bottom line (or lines) for you. You're the one who must live with your decision. And realize, too, that if you make a mistake -- if you choose a bottom line that turns out not to work for you -- *you can change it!*

None of us has totally pure motives, but it's crucial that you make decisions based on what's best for you. If you still secretly hope that you can somehow *maneuver* the alcoholic into sobriety, you're kidding yourself. Your decision must be *for you*, not for him -- *about you*, not about him.*

---

*Ask an alcoholism counselor about Intervention, a professionally directed program that can help an alcoholic into treatment.

NOTES

STEP SEVEN
Take Charge of Your Life

As you continue to work the previous six steps, appropriate decisions and actions will come as a logical and natural outgrowth of what you are learning. We are quick to acknowledge that this is a "selfish program", but by that we mean a program of *enlightened self-interest*. Rather than asking in a given situation, "How can I *fix* that?", you are, we hope, beginning to ask yourself, *"How do I choose to respond?"*

Strangely -- and wonderfully -- as you become more focused on your own needs and wants, you become willing to break the old destructive patterns that left you feeling bruised, worthless and hopelessly stuck. The more you take charge of your life, the more your self-esteem rises and the more willing you become to take responsible action *and to accept the consequences of your decisions.* You begin to know when to act and, just as important, when NOT to act; when to be silent, when to speak up; when to confront and when to walk away.

And you need not force detachment; you'll know it when it comes. IT FEELS DIFFERENT! Somehow that rigid self-control disappears and in its place there is a calm, secure sense of self -- a positive "I" feeling.

Be proud of your growth, but don't expect to become perfect. Oh yes, you *will* get caught in the alcoholic's web now and again. YOU'RE HUMAN. Be kind to yourself when it happens. You can say to yourself, with a little humor, "Oops, suckered again!" and then move on.

When the alcoholic behaves self-destructively (which may be most of the time), you no longer believe his rationalizations and excuses, because you see his illness for what it is. And yet somehow you no longer feel helplessly enmeshed in it. That's the difference. One day you'll find yourself saying something like: "I don't know how it happened, but he came home stinking drunk and I simply *wasn't afraid.* I didn't even want to tell him off. I told him I'd be home at eleven, put on my coat and left for my regular Al-Anon meeting."

In the broadest sense, these seven steps to detachment have nothing whatever to do with alcoholism. They are equally effective in helping you to assess *all* your relationships. Indeed, once you've learned the process of detachment, you may find yourself dealing with *everyone* in a more honest, realistic and productive way.

No one promises that you're going to walk off into some Hollywood sunset. Instead, these steps direct your path toward something far more enduring and satisfying. Do you recognize it now? It is the *real* miracle of personal growth. You are at last discovering YOU.

NOTES

AL-ANON'S TWELVE STEPS

* ONE *
We admitted we were powerless over alcohol -- that our lives had become unmanageable.

* TWO *
Came to believe that a Power greater than ourselves could restore us to sanity.

* THREE *
Made a decision to turn our will and our lives over to the care of God as we understood Him.

* FOUR *
Made a searching and fearless moral inventory of ourselves.

* FIVE *
Admitted to God, to ourselves, and to another human being the exact nature of our wrongs.

* SIX *
Were entirely ready to have God remove all these defects of character.

* SEVEN *
Humbly asked Him to remove our shortcomings.

* EIGHT *

Made a list of all persons we had harmed, and became willing to make amends to them all.

* NINE *

Made direct amends to such people wherever possible, except when to do so would injure them or others.

* TEN *

Continued to take personal inventory and when we were wrong promptly admitted it.

* ELEVEN *

Sought through prayer and meditation to improve our conscious contact with God as we understood Him, praying only for knowledge of His will for us and the power to carry that out.

* TWELVE *

Having had a spiritual awakening as a result of these steps, we tried to carry this message to others, and to practice these principles in all our affairs.

QUESTIONS FOR AN INVENTORY

DOES THE ALCOHOLIC:

1. have a personality change when drinking?
2. suffer memory lapses?
3. have problems at home, at work or socially because of drinking behavior?
4. cover up or protect drinking?
5. drink more before becoming intoxicated?
6. drink *less* before becoming intoxicated?

IS THE ALCOHOLIC:

7. making mistakes or having accidents (physical, auto, or mechanical) because or drinking?
8. losing time from duties or responsibilities?
9. angry and defensive about drinking?
10. sneaking or gulping drinks?
11. hiding bottles or cans?

OR IS IT THAT:

12. the drinking is bothering YOU?

SUGGESTED READING

AL-ANON'S TWELVE AND TWELVE
Al-Anon Family Groups, Inc.,
New York City, 1983

ALCOHOLICS ANONYMOUS
(A.A.'s "Big Book")
Alcoholics Anonymous,
New York City, 1976

THE ART OF SELFISHNESS
David Seabury: Pocket Books, 1964

THE BOOZE BATTLE
Ruth Maxwell: Ballantine Books, 1976

GETTING THEM SOBER
(Volumes I, II & Action Guide)
Toby Rice Drews:
Bridge Publishing, Inc., 1980

NEW PRIMER ON ALCOHOLISM
Marty Mann: Holt, Rinehart
& Winston, 1972

For an Up to Date
Catalog of Books
on All Aspects
of Alcoholism

THOMAS W. PERRIN, INC.
Post Office Box 190
Rutherford, New Jersey 07070

JUDITH M. KNOWLTON

Judy has a degree in Psychology from Oberlin College and her Master's in Group Process from Seton Hall University. A recovering alcoholic, she is a Certified Alcoholism Counselor with ten years' experience. Judy has been instrumental in starting several alcoholism programs in northern New Jersey. She is the founder of Action for Sobriety Groups, President of Quotidian, and the mother of three adult children. Her three cats are of varied sizes.

REBECCA D. CHAITIN

Becca is a writer and editor, part-time alcoholism counselor and recovering alcoholic. Born in Virginia, she is a graduate of Hollins College and worked for various New York publishers, including Time-Life Books, before she began free-lancing in the early 1970's. She now lives in Montclair, New Jersey with her three teenagers and three immense cats.

GIFTS OF GROWTH
also come at
discount when ordering
in quantity

QUOTIDIAN

The word means "recurring daily". (One day at a time!) The thistle symbolizes the disease of alcoholism: the sharp leaves are the active illness; the flower is the beauty of recovery. The flower is an amethyst (purple) color. The Greeks believed the amethyst could protect one from drunkenness - perhaps their idea of an easier, softer way?

QUOTIDIAN welcomes manuscripts (include SASE) on any aspect of alcoholism or personal growth.

PHONE NUMBERS

PHONE NUMBERS